Library of Congress catalog card number: 59-10958

Printed in the U.S.A.

C D E

LET'S FIND OUT

WHAT'S BIG

and

WHAT'S SMALL

by CHARLES and MARTHA SHAPP
pictures by VANA EARLE

FRANKLIN WATTS, INC.
575 Lexington Avenue, New York 22, N.Y.

Most of the time, it is easy to tell what's big.

An elephant is big.

A train engine is very big.

This airplane is very, very big.

The Empire State Building is very, very, very big.

Most of the time, it is easy to tell what's small.

A turtle is small.

A mouse is very small.

A butterfly is very, very small.

A bee is very, very, very small.

Sometimes it is not easy to tell what's big and what's small.

Is a rabbit big or small?
Let's find out.

Next to an elephant, a rabbit looks small.

Next to a mouse, a rabbit looks big.

Is a giraffe short or tall?
Let's find out.

Next to other animals, a giraffe looks
very tall.

Next to the Empire State Building, a giraffe looks very short.

Is a monkey big or small?
To find out, we must compare him
with other animals.

Who is tall?
Who is short?
To find out, we must compare.

Jack is shorter than his father.

But Jack is taller than

his sister Jill.

And Jill is taller than
the baby.

A bird looks big to a worm.

The bird looks small

to a cat.

To the cat, Jill looks like a giant.

Is this hat big or small?

Is the hat big?

Is the hat small?

"Ouch," says mother. "These shoes are too small."

Are the shoes big or small?

A thing looks small
when it is far away.

The same thing looks big
when it is near.

On the ground, a plane looks very big.

In the air, the same plane looks very small.

Most of the time, the big help the small.

Sometimes the small help the big.
The small tugboat helps the big
ocean liner.

Sometimes big things have small parts. The big

elephant 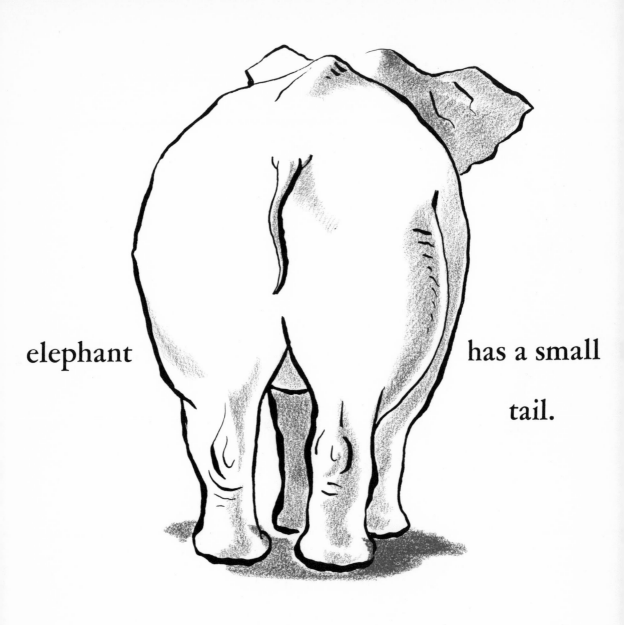 has a small

tail.

The big hippopotamus has

small ears.

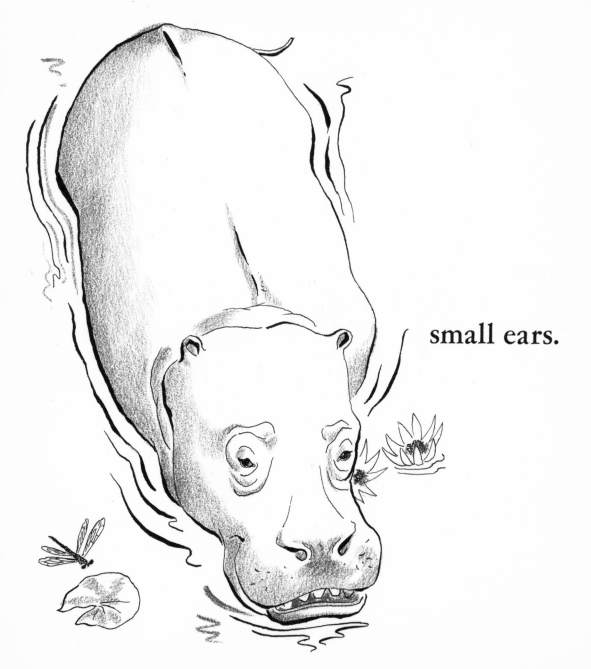

The small rabbit has big ears.

We must compare to find out:

What's big?

What's small?

 What's short?

What's tall?

VOCABULARY LIST

(Because these words are judiciously repeated in the text, they easily become part of the child's reading vocabulary.)

a
air
airplane
an
and
animals
are
away

baby
bee
big
bird
Building
but
butterfly

cat
compare

ears
easy
elephant
Empire
engine

far
father
find

giant
giraffe
ground

has
hat

have
help(s)
him
hippopotamus
his

in
is
it

Jack
Jill

let's
like
liner
looks

monkey
most
mother
mouse
must

near
next
not

ocean
of
on
or
other
ouch
out

parts

plane

rabbit

same
says
shoes
short(er)
sister
small
sometimes
State

tail
tall(er)
tell
than
the
these
thing(s)
this
time
to
too
train
tugboat
turtle

very

we
what's
when
who
with
worm